Grandpa's Oklahoma Farm
High on a Hill

By Juanita King

NEW FORUMS

Stillwater, Oklahoma

NEW FORUMS PRESS INC.

Published in the United States of America
by New Forums Press, Inc.1018 S. Lewis St.
Stillwater, OK 74074
www.newforums.com

Copyright © 2008 by New Forums Press, Inc.

All rights reserved. No part of this publication may be reproduced or
transmitted in any form or by any means, electronic or
mechanical, including photocopy, or any information storage
or retrieval system, without permission in writing from the
publisher.

Library of Congress Cataloging-in-Publication Data Pending

This book may be ordered in bulk quantities at discount from New
Forums Press, Inc., P.O. Box 876, Stillwater, OK 74076 [Federal
I.D. No. 73 1123239]. Printed in the United States of America.

ISBN 10: 1-58107-151-5
ISBN 13: 978-1-581071-51-1

Contents

About the Author ~ 5
1. The View from Grandpa's Farm ~ 9
2. The Skunk ~ 10
3. The Snake ~ 11
4. The Spider Web ~ 12
5. The Storm ~ 13
6. The Swallows ~ 14
7. Two Squirrels ~ 15
8. The Tea Party ~ 16
9. The Trio ~ 17
10. The Turtle ~ 18
11. The Unwanted Guest ~ 19
12. The New Born Calf ~ 20
13. The Old Rock House ~ 21
14. The Pickup Truck ~ 22
15. The Runaway Horse ~ 23
16. The Setting Sun ~ 24
17. The Backyard Pool ~ 25
18. The Calico Cat ~ 26
19. The Cedar Trees ~ 27
20. The Mimosa Tree ~ 28
21. The Morning Sun ~ 29
22. Playing in the Rain ~ 30
23. Shining Stars ~ 31
24. Thanksgiving on Grandpa's Farm ~ 33
25. Simple Things ~ 34
26. The Ant Hill ~ 35
27. Grandpa's Farm ~ 36
28. Grandpa's True Christmas Story ~ 40

29. I am So Blessed ~ 43
30. Little Hands ~ 44
31. Christmas at Grandpa's Farm ~ 46
32. Even a Kid Could Do It ~ 48
33. Family Treasures ~ 51
34. Grandma's Jewelry Box ~ 54
35. Grandma's Sheets ~ 55
36. A Little Girl's Thoughts ~ 56
37. Around the World on My Bicycle ~ 57
38. Building the Road ~ 58
39. Callie's Guest ~ 59
40. Nanny the Goat ~ 60
41. Our Over Night Guest ~ 61
42. The Mouse Trap ~ 62
43. The Move ~ 63
44. The Possum ~ 64
The Rest of the Story ~ 65

~~~~~~~~~~~~~~~~~~~~

Juanita with husband Woodrow, better known as Grandpa.

About the Author

Juanita King was born in Ponca City, Oklahoma, on December 1, 1925. She married Woodrow King in 1946. They moved to Jamaica as Missionaries in 1959. When they returned to the U.S. they moved to Cushing, Oklahoma, where they owned an operated a Dairy Queen for 15 years. During the years in Cushing she lived with her husband and three daughters on an 80 acre farm in a Spanish-Indian style home. This book is a window into life on this farm called "Kiora." Woodrow built the home, and barn, together they raised children, grandchildren, cattle, horses, dogs and cats there. Over the years Juanita has written stories/poems for friends and family based on day to day happenings. With encouragement from family and friends she has gathered some of her favorite stories/poems to share.

The poems in this book are a brief look into the life and people that resided there.... "On Grandpa's Farm-High On The Hill."

Juanita King

MEMORIES

My memories of the farm are oh so sweet
To keep them in a book, I thought, would be so neat
So with pen in hand and a cup of tea
I began to write my memories, all sweet to me
These memories cover many, many years
Writing them brought smiles and even some tears
As you grow older you too will see
Your own memories will bless you, as they have me

        Juanita King-2008

~A Special Thanks~

To our daughter Shannon Ree Hagan, for her prompting, support, and help in getting this book to the printers.

~~Dedication~~

This book is dedicated to the "grandpa" of my book, my husband of sixty-two years, Woodrow King. I appreciate all your encouragement and support and thank you for being a wonderful husband, father, and grandfather to our family.

The View from Grandpa's Farm

Grandpa knew what he had to do
He must buy a farm – with a wonderful view
When he saw 80 acres of native grass blowing in the wind
A thrill into Grandpa's heart it did send
He said I must buy that land for our farm
He did – and started building the barn
There were plans for the house to be built soon
A Mexican – Indian style with plenty of room
There was a pond – and fish added too
But the thing we enjoyed everyday was the beautiful view
To the Northeast was Cushing a small little town
To the Southwest, Highway 18 that wound around
To the Northwest is Stillwater where O.S.U. is found
And at night from our hill many lights abound
Lights from Agra, Perkins, and other small places
Shine like stars from heavenly spaces
You can see as far as 25 miles
When friends come to visit there are always smiles
To see such a view – almost takes our breath
So you see indeed we are blessed
To have this beauty of which most people just read
It belongs to us and we are grateful indeed
To see hills, valleys, grassy pastures, city lights and more
We are privileged to see as we step out our door
We see cattle, birds, wild deer and coyotes too
There are always new things to see and do
This beautiful memory remains with me still
Of the breathtaking view from
Grandpa's farm High on the hill

The Skunk

A terrible smell drifted through the open door
As we were leaving for school just as always before
We were stopped in our tracks by that awful smell
For Grandpa we began to yell
Well he came running and said with a smile
"Go on to school this will be here for a while"
In the corner of the porch was a fur ball black and white
"Yep!" Grandpa said "It's a skunk all right!"
We slipped out the door and hurried fast
We held our breath as the skunk we passed
When school was over and we had returned
For news of the skunk we all yearned
Grandpa said that the skunk had left during the day
Were we ever so glad he decided not to stay
We were glad he was gone but needless to say
The smell of that skunk lasted a few more days
This is a not so pleasant memory that remains with me still
From Grandpa's Farm High on The Hill

The Snake

Grandma was sitting out in the yard
Enjoying the rest because she was tired
The sun was hot and the breeze was cool
All the children had gone off to school
No one was around but Chez the dog
Watching a bug crawl over a log
While she was sitting in the shade out of the sun
A creature was crawling that would have ruined her fun
A huge black snake at least four feet long
Was crawling towards her where it didn't belong
But old faithful Chez from the corner of his eye
Would not let the big snake pass by
With a dash he grabbed that snake with his mouth
And shook it many times from North to South
When Grandma with a start glanced with her eyes
There a dead snake lay to her surprise
What a hero chez was our praise was no fake
Because he saved our Grandma from the bite of a snake
This memory remains with me still
On Grandpa's farm
High on the hill

The Spider Web

One summer morn just after a rain
I spied a thread like a silver chain
From the ground to a tree limb beside the door
Little did I know just what was in store
For my eyes to see as I stood on tip toe
Not knowing if I would encounter friend or foe
As the silver thread spiraled up to the sky
A beautiful shining web caught my eye
It looked like a palace with many rooms to see
And caught in the web was a tiny flea
The spider who wove the web was there
I had a feeling she had not played fair
As I looked at the beauty she did weave
With patterns and colors you could hardly believe
Now I believe the story of what is said
"Beware of being caught in the spider's web"
This picture of beauty remains with me still
On Grandpa's farm
High on the hill

The Storm

Dark skies, trees bending from a powerful wind
Lightening flashed as mighty noises it did send
The lightening flashed from East to West
As I clutched Grandpa's hand I did my best
To be brave as we looked at the stormy skies
But seeing the calmness in his eyes
I knew soon it would be over without any harm
For I felt safe
On Grandpa's farm
High on the hill

The Swallows

Outside on our veranda attached to the wall
Is a swallow's nest – that cannot fall
It was made years ago by a swallow so dear
And again and again it returns each year
From South America they return every spring
And the day they return makes my heart sing
They know the exact nest to return every year to
And they seem to know just what to do
They repair their nest and begin carrying straw
Back and forth carrying one at a time never tiring at all
Then they lay their eggs and set and wait
For the eggs to hatch – they are never late
Then one day we hear a tiny peep
As the world they begin to greet
Then as summer fades at the end of the day
We notice they have all flown away
We are sad at losing our friends so dear
But we know that they'll be back in the spring next year
Another scene that remains with me still
On Grandpa's farm
High on the hill

Two Squirrels

There is nothing as funny ever to see
As two squirrels playing in our Mulberry tree
One scampers up, and the other down
Then they circle each other going round and round
They hang by a foot and swish lazy bushy tails
They repeat this over and over all day without fail
You'd think they'd get tired and stop for a season
Why they act like they do is beyond all reason
This is one of the things we enjoyed to see
Two squirrels playing in our Mulberry tree
This memory remains with me still
On Grandpa's farm
High on the hill

The Tea Party

Of all the memories with Grandma,
One stands out to me
That is the times that we
Had our afternoon tea
She had bought me a tea set
From miles afar
Packed with tissue paper
In the back of the car
Tiny cups and saucers
With flowers of blue
And a tiny tea pot
That held tea for two
In the corner of the kitchen
Set an old stone jar with a lid
That was covered with a lace cloth
So the old jar was hid
It became a small table
With Victorian grace
For all you could see was the linen and lace
Little squares were cut from banana nut bread
They became tiny tea cakes with icing of blue and red
Like ladies of old we would sit and have tea
This was a pure delight for a little girl of three
This wonderful memory remains with me still
Tea party with Grandma, at Grandpa's farm
High on the hill

The Trio

There is a long twisted path that goes over the hill
My memories go back to that pathway still
I see Grandpa on his morning stroll
And a wonderful sight begins to unfold
Him walking with a stick in his hand
And behind him his critters like a marching band
First in line is old Chez faithful and true
Then Callie the cat behind a yard or two
If Grandpa stops for a few moments rest
Both the cat and dog do their very best
To just sit still and not move around
It's hard when birds fly by and bugs crawl on the ground
Butterflies flitter and turtles shuffling through
It's hard not to chase them or to grab at a few
When Grandpa gets rested then on they go
To watch these three is quite a show
Grandpa, the dog Chez, and Callie the cat
And from the window where I sat
To watch a scene my mind can't forget
Watching these three I will never regret
This memory too remains with me still
Setting at the window
On Grandpa's farm
High on the hill

The Turtle

On Grandpa's farm there's a big mulberry tree
Its limbs cover most of the yard – wonderful to see.
When the mulberries begin to fall on our hill
The birds come to eat their fill.
The sparrows – blue birds and black birds too
Many other birds – not just a few.
The tree is so old, so big, strong, and sound
Under a big root, there on the ground
Is a shelter wonderfully cool and dark
Protected by limbs that are covered with bark.
It is the home of Turtle, my friend, so slow.
He crawls along slowly with out any show
Just plodding along eating bugs in the sun
To watch him tuck in his head is so much fun
The hard shell on his back is covered with scars
From crawling under roots and barbed wire with the jolts
    and jars
From the hoofs of cows running over him
You would think they could see the state he is in.
He has to walk so slow and he's not very tall
But nobody seems to care at all
But under that tree is his haven of rest
And this is the place that he likes the best
After each day of looking for food in fields of hay
He slowly heads for his home at the end of each day
We make sure no rocks or sticks cover his door
Each night he comes in just as the night before
Slowly, slowly, plodding along
As if nothing in the world was wrong
He blinks his eyes and looks at me
As if to say "Thank you for my home under this tree"
This is a sweet memory that remains with me still
At Grandpa's farm
High on the hill

The Unwanted Guest

One day when the back door was open wide
A visitor, unwanted crawled right inside
He sneaked in quietly and we didn't see
How he escaped our eyes is still a mystery
That evening when Grandpa was walking down the hall
In a loud voice "Come Quick" he began to call
Come see what's laying here on the floor
There was a three foot snake by the dining room door
There he was all curled up taking a nap
We knew to this visitor we could not adapt
He woke up and crawled behind the china against the wall
With fear and haste we ran to the phone and made a call
For help from two very good friends
Grandpa said "Don't let him crawl out, keep an eye on him"
When the friends arrived and the china moved out
They shot him and we all began to shout
There would have been no sleeping that night in our beds
With the thought of a snake going through our heads
After ice cream and cake with our friends that night
We went to bed knowing everything was all right
This scary memory remains with me still
At Grandpa's farm
High on the hill

The New Born Calf

I went with Grandpa to see the new born calf
As I watched it try to stand it made me laugh
Its legs were trembling, all wobbly and spread
Its hair was wet and curly from its tail to its head
Large brown eyes and very big ears
I laughed and laughed until it brought tears
It would try to stand and fall flat on its tummy
This happened many times, it was so funny
Then after awhile it began to feel
It was ready for its first meal
It nudged its mother and began to nurse
It sucked and sucked until it almost burst
Then it lay in the sun to rest a while
Then Grandpa took my hand with a great big smile
And he ask me if I'd like the calf to be mine
Oh yes! I said, "That would be fine!"
I remember seeing my first baby calf still
On Grandpa's farm
High on the hill

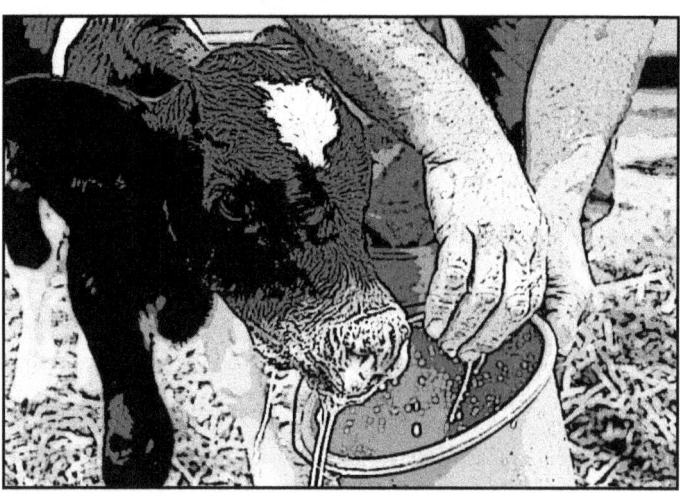

The Old Rock House

Across the road from Grandpa's farm
Sets an old rock house, a shed, and a barn
In the back field the grasses sway in the wind
In front, the wild flowers their sweet smell sends
A delightful odor, that floats over the hills
It seems all the countryside the aroma fills
The old house sits so lonely and quiet, doors hanging ajar
Five gables pierce the clouds in the sky afar
In and out the windows birds fly to and fro
And late at night the fireflies are aglow
They circle the old house in twinkling flames
As if they are playing tiny fairy games
In the day time the old rock house sits very still
Not very far from our house on the hill
It reminds me of stories of days gone by
Of families who lived there and the children's delightful
    cries
While playing in the yard – not a care in the world
This beautiful picture in my mind's eye unfurls
Then on stormy nights with lightening flashing
The rain pouring down and the thunder clashing
As we peek out our windows to take a look
The old grey house looking like a picture in a mystery book
What once was a cheery and beautiful home
Now stands so sad and all alone
Yet still refusing to be destroyed by the years
As I look at the scene my eyes fill with tears
This is another memory that remains with me still
As we viewed the old rock house from Grandpa's farm
High on the hill

The Pickup Truck

The old orange and tan truck like an armored car
Carried trash, hauled cattle both near and far
Hauled feed and bundles of hay
Sometimes it sat in the hot sun all day
It sat out in the rain, hail, snow and sleet
Grandpa would let us ride on the tailgate and dangle our
    feet
From the back of the pickup – what pure joy
This was such fun for each girl and boy
Many times we traveled from the house to the barn
Sitting in the back of that pickup
On Grandpa's farm
High on the hill

The Runaway Horse

On top of Cherokee running like the wind
I realized just what trouble I was in
I could hardly hold on or stay in the saddle
To get him to stop was really a battle
But our old dog Chez got in front of me
For he saw the limb of a huge oak tree
Old Chez kept me from getting knocked off that horse
So I'll always be grateful to him of course
This memory truly remains with me still
On Grandpa's farm
High on the hill

The Setting Sun

Grandpa was tired from stacking the hay
The children were weary from the hot sun and play
Grandma had finished her chores for the day
And came outside and stared to say
"Children it's time to come eat and rest"
When all eyes noticed the setting sun in the West
As if it was slowly going over the hill
The picture it made gave us a thrill
A huge orange ball slowly, slowly descending
A wonderful scene and thrill
As it was slowly hidden behind the hill
As we all stood and watched holding our breath
That God would let our eyes be blessed
We are so happy we didn't miss
Such a glorious sight as this
The memory remains with me still
From Grandpa's farm
High on the hill

The Back Yard Pool

When spring is over and there is no more school
I still think of Grandpa's farm and the back yard pool
It was plastic and only 18 inches deep
But we used to jump in with a great big leap
As if it were Olympic size
Pretending the diving board was oh so high
In the hot sun we would splash and play
Drinking Kool-Aid and swimming all day
Old Chez the dog stood watching so sad
Wanting to jump in with us so bad
We would play games of lets pretend
Thrilling moments to our day send
These memories remain with me still
On Grandpa's farm
High on the hill

The Calico Cat

On Grandpa's farm there's a calico cat
She's not real skinny – not too fat
She has a coat of black and orange fur
When she sits in the sun you can hear her purr
A pillow of fur so cuddly and soft
She sleeps in the barn up high in the loft
She keeps all the rats and mice out of the barn
She's an adorable pet here on the farm
This too is a memory that remains with us still
From Grandpa's Farm High on the hill

The Cedar Trees

Cedar trees grow on Grandpa's farm
Down by the pond and in back of the barn
You can smell the cedar all around
Sometimes you can find tiny baby trees popping up from the
    ground
But the most wonderful time to see the trees
Is when the winter comes and in the breeze
The limbs sway covered with snow
And in the winter sun they glisten and glow
With icicles hanging gleaming so bright
When I look our my window it really is a sight
A beautiful village of cedar trees
And when the temperature falls and it begins to freeze
The change from green to white
And in my memory this beautiful sight
After all these years remains with me still
On Grandpa's farm
High on the hill

The Mimosa Tree

The first thing planted on Grandpa's farm
Was a Mimosa tree just west of the barn
It was small and straggly not much to see
But we knew that someday it would be a big tree
Through all the sunshine, sleet and snow
We watched with joy that mimosa tree grow
One day we noticed with squeals of glee
Thousands of beautiful pink blossoms all over the tree
This memory too remains with me still
On Grandpa's farm
High on the hill

The Morning Sun

One morning while leaning on my window sill
I saw a breath taking beauty that gave me a thrill
A huge orange ball rose up in the sky
And in the next few moments that passed by
I saw the morning bathed in a golden glow
As the birds sang and the rooster began to crow
The cows mooed while eating their hay
Contented to be starting such a beautiful day
The suns rays swept over all the farm
With a wonderful glow from the pond to the barn
I stood so still and watched enchanted
As the beautiful picture in my mind was planted
The huge orange ball rose slowly in the sky
So beautiful and bright it blinded my eyes
This golden moment remains with me still
From my bedroom window
On Grandpa's farm
High on the hill

Playing in the Rain

The day was hot and there was nothing to do
The sun was shining in the sky so blue
All the children's faces were gloomy and sad
Not because they were being punished for being bad
It was one of those days which were only a few
When there simply was nothing to do
When all of the sudden there was a dark cloud in the North
And big drops of rain began to come forth
A few drops at first then ten thousand more
And Grandma came and stood by the door
Get your bathing suits on and you can play
Out in the rain for the rest of the day
Well, we jumped and we ran, we shouted and screamed
While on our body the drops of rain gleamed
Such fun we had all afternoon
When the rain stopped it was all too soon
The memories of playing in the rain remain with me still
While at Grandpa's farm
High on the hill

Shining Stars

All the family was sitting out in the yard
I remember grandpa was feeling very tired
Not much excitement going on
And the day had been so very long
Fixing the fences so the cows couldn't wander
Fighting the rain and a very loud thunder
But the sky had cleared and supper was over
As we sat in the yard we could smell the fresh clover
The smell was so sweet and the breeze was cool
It was almost nine and it was a rule
To say our prayers and sleep for the night
But as we looked at the sky we saw such a sight
The stars began to shine a million or more
Oh! Yes! We had seen them many times before
But each time was special as we watched them glisten
And again to Grandpa's story we would sit and listen
How the stars could guide you the Big Dipper too
If you were lost and without a clue
As to direction and which way was best
To go North, South, East, or West
Using the stars Grandpa said you could find your way
And we always believed everything Grandpa had to say
This memory of shining stars remains with me still
In the front yard at Grandpa's farm
High on the hill

Thanksgiving on Grandpa's farm

The memories of Thanksgiving on the farm will always remain
Each year was special, regardless of sunshine, sleet, snow, or rain
Grandpa and Grandma greeting us as we arrived at the door
The sweet smell of turkey cooking, dressing, pumpkin pie and more
Cranberry Salad, Grandma's noodles cooked in turkey broth
The Thanksgiving table set with Grandma's gold tablecloth
With pewter plates and goblets, used every Thanksgiving Day
When all were seated around the table, with heads bowed to pray
To thank God for the Pilgrims, their true story we were told
About the hardships they suffered, and the winters so cold
Then we thanked God for our food and another Thanksgiving Day
For our family, food and friends, America and the freedom to pray
Afternoon was spent with Grandpa in his chair with eyes closed
Unaware of all the noise around him, peacefully he dozed
The voices of the children playing outside in the cold
Braving the strong wind, freezing snow, so bold
Taking turns to pet the cows, and ringing the bell
So many things they did, we could begin to tell
When evening came, with all inside warming by the fire
Another meal at the table again was everyone's desire
These Thanksgiving memories remain with us still
On Grandpa's Farm High on the Hill

Simple Things

Silver and gold an all that it brings
Are not as wonderful as simple things
Like a child playing in the sun
Skipping rope or seeing them run
In wild abandonment, not a care in the world
Like watching a beautiful flower its petals unfurl
These memories of our children remain with us still
From Grandpa's Farm - High on the Hill

The Ant Hill

On Grandpa's farm beside the fence of railroad ties
By a clump of grass an ant hill lies
I spied it one morning on my way to the barn
Decided to stand and watch – couldn't do any harm
Thousands of little ants were going to and fro
Yet seemingly knowing just where to go
To get food – bits and pieces of insects and grain
They worked all day in sunshine and rain
Everyday doing just as before
Getting ready for winter their food to store
Each one seemed to know what to do, and when
Working together, like very good friends
Small ants, so little – yet working so hard
Like a tiny factory of workers right in our back yard
Each one doing their part to gain
Food for winter away from snow and rain
One tiny ant struggled, pulled and tugged
At a large insect – a beetle bug
Larger than he by four times or more
But he finally got the bug in the ant hill door
This memory of the ant hill remains with me still
On Grandpa's farm
High on the hill

Grandpa's Farm

Grandpa's farm is high on a hill
Each time I visit, there's always a thrill
I can see hills and valleys for miles around
Each day there are new things to see, I've found
The cattle grazing in the fields of hay
Or a little calf that has gone astray
The neighbors' horses galloping over the hill
I can see their manes flying in the breeze still
I can see the water tower on a nearby farm
A crow perched on top away from all harm
Rows of tiny birds sitting on the telephone lines
Like a heavenly choir chirping in time
No matter if the sun is rising or going down
The beauty is glorious and wonderful I've found
I can see the pond off to the East
The memories of that pond will never cease
It brings back thoughts of afternoon swims,
Beetle bugs and turtles crawling around on the rim

Fish flipping and flopping tails in the air
Playing all day long without a care
There are walnut trees down by the pond
The nuts of which I am so fond
The pecan trees that grown this side of the hill
Picking and cracking for Grandma's candy was a thrill
The wild persimmon grove where I spent many an hour
Tasting fruit that was still quite sour
The clumps of redbud tress growing
With vibrant shades of pink bestowing
The cedar, juniper, and dogwood trees,
You never saw such an array as all of these
There were blackjack, hackberry, and poplar trees
Maple, oak, and mimosa with leaves blowing in the breeze
The blue stem, Indian, and Buffalo grass waving in the
    breeze
As if all nature they were trying to tease
Yes, all those grasses are native you see
In an era gone by – living history to me
There are fences built by Grandpa on a hot summer day
A place to separate, feed, or just gaze at his cattle every day
The cows, even the bull, they all knew me
Because Grandpa took me with him to feed you see
The maternity pen for his new momma cows
Where a new baby calf would our excitement arouse
Grandpa once had goats and horses too
But as he got older he had to get rid of a few
I cannot leave out Kiora the bull, Sam and Chief too
These were Grandpa's other dogs faithful and true
Chief would follow him where ever he went
And even kill a snake when he was sent
At the North end of the barn was a special factor
For under its roof sat the old grey tractor
I'll never forget the days I sat on Grandpa's lap
Off we went followed by Chez and Callie the cat
We rode to the North and then to the West
This was some of the times that I loved best
Grandma's last words were "You two take care"
But with Grandpa there was nothing to fear

The motor was loud and we had to shout
What each other said was always in doubt
With Grandpa holding on tight to me
High on his lap everything I could see
Then one day he said "You take the wheel"
The thrill of that moment made my head reel
To drive that old tractor was my hearts desire
Even though half a mile was not all that far
I'll always remember that day with a smile
It was the first day I drove my very first half mile
Out back of the house was a mulberry tree
We spent many hours under its branches my cousins and me
We would run and play hide and seek
Stopping only to listen to the woodpeckers beat
There was a fence around the house of railroad ties
Behind which on summer days you could hear the cries
Of the grandchildren playing and laughing all day
On bicycles, tricycles, and jump ropes with hair all array
Playing and laughing with shouts of glee
Not a care in the world feeling so free
We would be awakened some nights by an eerie yell
Was it wild dogs or coyotes we couldn't tell
One day a doe came in the yard
So very gentle yet still on her guard
Her big round eyes saying who are you?
As if to say I am a child too
But one move of our arm or a look to the right
Quickly she bound over the hill and out of sight
I remember the turtles that came to be fed
We used to watch them tuck in their little heads
They would each year wait for the mulberries to fall
And one by one they would eat them all
Oh the bliss of sitting under the Mulberry tree
Sipping lemonade it always excited me
Crawling by our toes would be a beetle bug
On the blanket of grass that was like a huge green rug
We dug for worms and had water fights
We helped hang on the house the Christmas lights
Made candy, read stories, and trimmed the Christmas tree

Helped wrap Christmas packages for all to see
No room for sadness or an alarm
For all was secure on Grandpa's farm
We would hear Grandma call "Come get some food"
But time was short and we were not in the mood
We were hungry but time was flying by
And we wanted to sit and look at the sky
When the day was over with the setting sun
There was no stopping our day of fun
As the night grew dark and all the stars glistened
To Grandpa's tales of the galaxy we would listen
He told of Jupiter, of Mars and the Big Dipper
This was more thrilling to us than stories of Flipper
All was dark the night was still
We had played and laughed and ate our fill
As we said our prayers we thanked God for the day
Then there was nothing else left to say
Little bodies were weary wanting to sleep
As we were tucked into our beds sinking into the deep
The memories of all these things remain with us still
When we were at Grandpa's farm
High on the Hill

Grandpa's True Christmas Story

On Christmas Eve when all is still and serene
After the story of Christ's birth with tree lights agleam
Grandpa tells another true story that is exciting to me
It's the story of Christmas 1943
The memory will forever be with me
During World War II, in the middle of the sea
We were fighting for America – Land of the Free
When at four a.m. without any warning
A torpedo hit our ship this Christmas morning
One end was sinking fast in the morning dawn
Life boats were lowered while trying to stay calm
One of the falls broke – amid all the shouts

Then "Man Overboard"! The call rang out
On a sinking ship it's each man for him self you see
The Captain said it was up to me
To save the man or leave him to die
I knew in my heart I had to try
To go over the side and save this man
I must try to do all that I can
The water was so deep – the night was pitch black
And at any moment sharks or the enemy could attack
I finally got the man into the boat
While other's around us began to float
In life boats filled to the brim
All knowing the danger we were in
Mules we were transporting put up a valiant fight
Having to watch them die in the sea was such a sad sight
We saw the ship was sinking fast
But all the crew was in the boats at last
The days and nights slowly passed
We had rationed our water down to the last
In the Indian Ocean we drifted, the days were so hot
After two days and two nights an English corvette we did
    spot
When the ill sunburned bodies were moved on board
The land of India we sailed toward
We were taken by the English moving so slow
As we had some rough miles inland to go
We were taken to an Indian camp to wait
Until word was sent to American of our fate
Our families at home heard that we were dead
At least that was what the report to them said
All the food we had were coconuts and bananas
We didn't know when or even if they would find us
At night we slept on pads made of bark and around us a net
Keeping out snakes and wild hyenas, and to our regret
We had no way of reporting we were there
Everyday at the horizon we would stare
Hoping to see someone coming to rescue us
So heavenward we aimed our prayers and trust
Through a breakdown in all communications

The message from the English ship never reached our nation
For three months we lived on that shore
Then again we were picked up by the English and traveled
    some more
We were taken in slow moving cattle cars
On this long trip with jolts and jars
To the Southern tip of India to board a boat
Then to Colombo, Ceylon we did float
Where an English recuperation home for soldiers had been
    built
We Americans enjoyed their hospitality without any guilt
After many weeks we finally got passage with a survivors
    pass
And the shores of America we saw at last
How thankful I am that God saw me through
Dangers, hardships, and hunger, so that years later I could
    be with you
The memory of Grandpa's Christmas story remains with me
    still
From Grandpa's Farm
High on the Hill

I Am So Blessed

This morning I heard a mocking bird sing
And watched a humming bird feed, such a tiny small thing
I saw the ants hurrying to and fro
To fill their storehouse in the earth below
Storing food for family and friends
Knowing that summer always ends
I saw Callie the cat cleaning her fur
With her tiny pink tongue not missing a purr
A butterfly flew slowly by me
Orange and black wings so beautiful to see
 I watched a tiny lady bug, a caterpillar, and a turtle
Playing in the shade of Grandma's crepe myrtle
The sparrow eating on Grandpa's plums
The bees swarming around the giant pink mums
A hawk above flew slowly by, dipping its wings
While on the tree limb the whip-r-will sings
The sound of Grandma doing her chores
The swing and creak of the wooden back door
As she hangs out the laundry on the line to dry
Blowing in the breeze under the pale blue sky
I feel so blessed as I wander among the redbud trees
Listening to the buzz of the bumble bees
Grandpa sitting straight on the tractor seat
Hauling hay from the barn for the cows to eat
I am so blessed to see such beauty and feel such a thrill
As I visit Grandpa's farm
High on the hill

Little Hands

One of the most precious memories that I remember still
Are the "little hands" that visited our farm on the hill
There were little hands covered with dirt
Little hands wiping catsup on a Sunday shirt
A little hand holding a turtle he had just found
Or a tiny bug picked up off the ground
The tears of a little girl with bird nest in hand
With a broken egg covered with sand
Little hands stroking the fur of Callie the cat
Or just giving her a gentle smack
For scratching a leg or arm
Wanting to scold her but to do her no harm
Little hands helping Grandpa spread hay
Wanting to do their part for the day
Little hands accidentally breaking Grandpa's tomato vine
Then with a toothless grin saying "sorry" just in time
A hand flying a kite with an upturned face
Beautiful enough for a front page to grace
Little hands clutching your skirt in times of fear
Little hands brushing away a sudden tear
Little hands bringing in a worm found in the earth
Little hands clutching your finger right after birth
Little hands reaching out for a cookie or a toy
Little hands so precious of each girl and boy
Little hands working a puzzle on the old marble table
Little hands doing things that they were not really able
Little hands doing chores on Grandpa's farm
Little hands holding a ball of Grandma's yarn
Little hands reaching to hold you tight
A little hand holding yours in the dark of night
Little hands tightly griping the old rope swing
With merry laughter I can still hear ring
Little hands helping Grandpa plant the garden in the spring
Little hands trying on Grandma's golden wedding ring

Little hands opening the gate for cows to come in
So proud to help even in the cold winter wind
Little hands driving the tractor on Grandpa's lap
Little hands in the wind clutching a little fur cap
Little hands helping the cake to mix
Or helping Grandpa the broken chair to fix
Little hands tying a shoe for the very first time
Pulling a wooden toy – or finding a dime
Little hands running a comb through Grandpa's hair
While he was sitting half asleep in his old leather chair
Little hands clapping with sounds of joy
With giggles and laughter from each girl and boy
But my favorite memory of little hands I see
Are the little ones pressed together at night praying with
    Grandpa and me
This blessed memory remains with me still
From Grandpa's Farm High of the Hill

Christmas at Grandpa's Farm

Christmas will always be special to me
Not for the expensive presents or the lights I see
But special memories of days gone by
The birth of Jesus and the star in the sky
Without his birth we could not still
Celebrate Christmas at the farm high on the hill
When we were small we could hardly wait
To see the farm and Grandpa's gate
The snow on the trees, house, and in the yard
Made it look like a giant Christmas card
When the front door opened we could smell the turkey and
    cake
Along with all the other things Grandma had baked
There would be candy, homemade bread and pies
All the Christmas decorations were beautiful to our eyes
The stockings were hung for each child there
Filled with small toys and candy with tender care

The tall evergreen filled with ornaments and lights
Was surrounded by packages wrapped in colors so bright
Tied with ribbons and bows, silver, green and red
Visions of what they held filled each child's head
Christmas cards were in a basket, sitting on the floor
A chili pepper wreath hung on the door
Dinner was ready, Grandmother called us to eat
Carving the turkey for Grandpa was quite the feat
With bowed heads thanks was given for the birth of God's son
That made this holiday possible, with the food, gifts and fun
After dinner was over we would pause for awhile
Open packages and see the gifts that were given each child
There were trucks, socks, story books and balls
And for the little girls sweet baby dolls
There were sweaters, scarves, and mittens too
There were all kinds of games and puzzles to do
Perfume, makeup and handkerchiefs of lace
Lots of laughter, with smiles on each face
There were games inside, but outside too
Some played in the snow or just enjoyed the view
Little girls dressed and fed their dolls with motherly care
While Grandpa dozed in this big leather chair
The evening always came hours too soon
We would all pitch in to help clean up the room
Papers and boxes went in the fireplace to be burned
For more hours in the day we all yearned
At last it was time for Grandpa's Christmas story
How he fought in World War II for peace and Old Glory
Every Christmas was special with memories still
Of Grandpa's Farm
High on the hill

Even A Kid Could Do It!!

Woodie said come on now Juanita, I need you today
It's just a small job and you'll get some pay
Now Imogene helps Joe and Donna helps Bill
They're out all the time, their trailers to fill,
Or cutting out cows, or feeding some hay
Regardless of the weather – freezing, sunny or gray
Now this isn't a big job – a small kid would do
But you are my wife and I'd rather have you!
Well the day was cold and the wind blew hard
But he said "Oh it's easy – you won't get tired"
So I put on some long johns – a wool cap on my head
Gloves, ear muffs, a scarf and a coat as heavy as lead
High top boots, too big for my feet
And Woodie's coveralls – to big in the seat
We got out to the pen and he pointed out
Ear tags, color, gender, and what the job was about
Well, I could see right away – this was no small thing
I began to wonder what a mistake might bring
Right off the bat- I closed the gate wrong
The wind grew colder and the minutes grew long
He said "I need these cows in the trailer before night"
"All will go well if you'll just do everything right!"
"Now head off that cow – she's the one I really need!"
"All will go well if my instructions you'll heed"
She ran right towards me, eyes glaring, looking like a
      dragon!
These feet of mine they weren't laggin!
I ran for the fence – and left that gate open!
Out into the pasture that cow went a loppin!!
Woodie shook his head and said "Oh My!"
A kid could have done it! You didn't even try!
I could see by his eyes, he was a little put out.
I said "That cow will come back, without a doubt
Let's go on to another – which one goes in now?"

He pointed and said "That three year old cow
The one with the white patch right on her head"
But he never said which one the black or the red
Now the trailer was hooked up to the head gate and all
"Hurry it up!" Grandpa yelled "We can't wait til next fall."
That cow ran straight for the trailer – after a whack on the
    nose
Too slowly I moved, I was frozen down to my toes
That cow made a dash to the left and then out of sight
Woodie shook his head and shouted – "We'll never get this
    done tonight!"
Right then and there he threw no small fit
And repeated again, "Even a kid could do it!"
We ran those cows to the right and to the left
Woodie was getting more and more out of breath
He said "Juanita, what's the matter with you?"
But it was those crazy cows, he should blame them too!

He said, "Go get some cubes – OK, hay would do,
We'll rest a few minutes and feed a few
I got into the barn – the door banged shut
Out ran the cat with a hiss and strut
I stepped on the pitchfork and banged my head
Said my last prayer – thinking I was surely dead
Woodie said "Com on now, pitch out that hay"
I said "Just wait! Rome wasn't built in a day!!"
With a knot on my forehead and feet icy cold
I was ready to quit – so I really got bold!
I told Woodie "Those cows all look the same!"
He said "They've all got ear tags, Juanita, they even have
    names!
Now open that gate and the trailer door
Move out three cows and I'll move in some more."
The last cow ran by – kicked me in the shin
Now this didn't help the mood I was in!
Those cow tails were swishing to and fro
The right direction those cows didn't want to go!
Finally with head throbbing and heart racing fast
The very last cow into the trailer, in front of me passed,
I was proud of my help – for it took some grit
Woodie just walked away mumbling "Even a kid could do
    it!"
This uncomfortable memory remains with me still
From Grandpa's Farm High on the Hill

Family Treasures

In Grandma's house high on the hill
There were rooms that special furniture did fill
Some day they will be sold or given away
But the memories live in our heads to stay
Grandma's china cabinet covers the dining room wall
With many shelves – it's so great and tall
The jug collection, Wedge wood plates trimmed with gold,
Tiny cups from England – their history unfolds
Great Grandma's berry dish, the pewter collection
The silver platter, where we could see our reflection
The carved bone bottle opener from Great Grandpa's store
And many other old dishes galore
The mahogany table in the corner that holds the silver tea
    set
That always shone so bright, I can see it yet
Bright and shiny, so beautiful to see
Ready to serve the afternoon tea
The marble top table with legs of gold
So cool to the touch many puzzles it did hold
As we were seated around to piece together
All kinds of puzzles in all kinds of weather
The old chopping block in the kitchen it stands
Use to be in the old hotel, used by many hands
The hundred year old brass bowls in the corner they gleam
In England they held the cow's milk and the cream
The teapots in all shapes, sizes, colors and ages
Their history could fill many, many pages
The Tiffany lamp beside my bed
Sheds light on the pillow that holds my head
As I look up through the beautiful colored glass
Like a fairy tales palace – but alas!!
I would fall asleep with little care
Knowing that the memory would always be there
The four-poster bed so stately and tall
Pushed into the corner up against the wall

Hours were spent playing on top and even under the bed
So high we never worried about hitting our head
When we were small and friends came overnight to stay
Many times for hours we would play
The bed became a castle, fort, and a tent for camping out
I will never forget all the giggles and the shouts
Of children playing the whole afternoon
It seemed night time always came too soon
Then at night it became a haven of rest
It was made by hand by a freed slaves' son
Brought from Jamaica by ship, for it weighed a ton
The grandfather's clock made in 1776
With the other antiques, very well it did mix
We could hear through the night the tick tock, tick tock
A giver of time that old tall clock
The hall tree with the mirror held grandpa's hats and gloves
Reflected the faces of the grandchildren he loves
The old bookcase in the room upstairs
With a curved glass door that was very rare
It held old books and other things through the years
Withstood all the family fears
Of the glass being broken from being opened and shut many
    times
But it's still intact with just a few scratches and lines
Old books by Zane Grey, read over and over again
Old Mark Twain books we could never lend
The Indian peace pipe, hanging over the fireplace
The round dinning room table where over each meal we
    said grace
The bentwood chairs all scratched and worn
Made many years before we were born
The butter mold and the old round churn
Grandma said she use to hide instead of taking her turn
To churn the cream into butter each day
Because she would rather go outside and play
In every room my eyes can see
The beautiful things that hold so many memories for me
Some very old, cracked, withered and worn
Used many, many years before I was born
The old walnut dresser, with marble top, grey

It mirrored many faces for many a day
The old square trunk that held trinkets of old
Not much to look at, but it holds memories worth gold
Like Grandpa's first little hand made suite
When wearing it he felt so proud and thought he looked so cute
Made of plain cotton material, red and white in color
In his day to make it, it probably cost a dollar
For those were the days of five-cent ice cream
And a piece of stick candy was every child's dream
The tiny Bentwood rocker, with the broken arm
Oh! But it still holds a special charm
It's hard to imagine Grandpa's feet hardly touching the floor
Until you remember that he was only four
The brass finger bowls from India far away
Gleaming on the mantle always brightened the day
The Navajo rug hanging on the wall
And family pictures lining the hall
The black ebony elephants, a gift from a friend so dear
With the tiniest baby elephant bringing up the rear
The little nannies chair at the foot of Grandma's bed
Where in England, babies were tenderly held and fed
With its short legs, the reason is said
In case the nannies dropped the babies on their head
The old barometer hanging on the wall
With the crack on the face, it's still loved by all
Captain Herron, an old friend gave it to us
When we lived in Jamaica, without a fuss
He said "It's a gift, from me a friend,
So you memories of me will never end"
All the Indian artifacts bring memories of days gone by
And as I view and touch these things I sigh
The branding iron from the 101 Ranch so great
To many, many cows this was their fate
The old brass fire screen we see every day
Stands next to the wall out of the way
Living with all these old things our life has been so blessed
For all these memories remain with me still
From Grandma and Grandpa's farm-
High on the hill

Grandma's Jewel Box

I always remember Grandma's jewel box
It wasn't made of gold, silver, or wood it didn't even have a
    lock
It wasn't tied with leather or a gold cord
It was an ordinary shoe box of heavy cardboard
Many times when there wasn't anything to do
Grandma would say "come" I've something to show you
We can look in "the box" and our eyes would get big and
    wide
For we all knew the things it held inside
We loved to hold the tiny elephant of real ivory
It was brought back by Grandpa, from India in 1943
There was a bracelet and earrings of beaten silver
Its threads so thin
Cameos from Italy and rings from places Grandpa had been
But of all the jewels, necklaces, brooches and rings
We loved the best to see the Indian things
We could try on the rings with stones of blue
The Concho belts, the bracelets and necklaces old and new
We would count the nuggets on the long silver threads
Try on rings and bracelets made of coral, red
We would play like we had a store with jewels so fine
And before we knew it there was no more time
Hours had passed by as we played "let's pretend" with
    Grandma's things
She well knew the pleasure her Jewel Box would bring
She would smile and say "Time to put them away"
And in the box they would all go – waiting for another day
When we would again look inside the "Jewel Box"
A shoe box of cardboard without any lock
That took us to far countries – and into many lands
We were Queens, dancing ladies, and runaways in Gypsy
    Bands
This wonderful memory remains with me still
Of Grandma's Jewel Box at Grandpa's farm
High on the hill

Grandma's Sheets

As I climbed into bed each night for sleep so sweet
I remember the wonderful smell of Grandma's sheets
The smell, like the breeze blowing over the hill
Like a wind blowing, sometimes strong or sometimes still
And the smell of the farm all the things I adored
Things only nature could afford
I would fall asleep dreaming of far off lands
And wake to the smell of sheets folded by Grandma's hands
As they covered me as I laid so still
And thought of the joy of visiting Grandpa's farm
High on the hill

A Little Girls Thoughts

When I was just a little girl
I pondered what I would be
A princess- A queen – a Movie Star
Or even a pilot, flying so free
As the years passed, I finished school
Became a wife, and a mother of three
I thought back over my life so far
And decided I was happy just being me
This thought stays with me still
As Grandpa and I live happily
High on the hill

Around The World on My Bicycle

In front of the house on Grandpa's farm
In a driveway that curls like a giant arm
While on my bicycle playing lets pretend
I circle the world with out an end
Going round and round I travel to many places
Hear foreign voices and see many faces
Pretending I'm a great cyclist with legs of steel
Fatigue or tiredness I would never feel.
As I ride round the circle on Grandpa's farm
High on the hill

Building the Road

The huge big machine – making so much noise
Was something to watch for each girl and boy
They were building a road in front of Grandpa's farm
We stood afar off watching away from all harm
Bringing in tons of sand, stone and oil was their duty
To make this blacktop road a thing of beauty
Cars use to get stuck in the mud when going to and fro
Now they whiz by as to town they go
The sight of the road builders remain with me still
In front of Grandpa's farm
High on the hill

Callie's Guest

Callie our cat is getting very old-As you can plainly see for sure
She sleeps on our veranda now-The cold nights she can hardly endure
So we made her a house out of a box-And set it on a table by the front door
She would just sit most of the day in the sun -Or roam around the yard and explore
At night when it gets very cool-As nights are, high on our hill
She would crawl into her little box house-I can see her sitting there still
A ball of calico fur so soft -A purr like soft music to hear
Poor Callie, she was getting old – to us she was so dear
She seemed to like her little box house - Inside each night she would rest
After washing her face and licking her paws-To look pretty, she would try her best
Then one night when we came home - Callie was lying on the cold porch floor
As we looked into her little box house- A new face was inside the door
A friendly possum had come to call - and eaten Callie's food and then decided to stay
She had crawled into Callie's house and fallen a sleep -A good place to rest at the end of the day
So Callie, great cat that she was – shared her warm house that night for a good cause
We knew she was special but for this she deserved much applause
This is a memory that lingers still
From Grandpa's farm
High on the hill

Nanny the Goat

We had a goat named Nanny- she had a peculiar mind
When milking her you had to feed her from a bowl with a shine
Well Grandpa didn't know this until it was too late
One morning at milking time – a kick was to be his fate
Well you can rest assured - that kick changed his frame of mind
Each milking time from that day on – she ate from a bowl with a mighty shine
We all laugh at this memory still
Of Grandpa milking that goat on Grandpa's Farm High on the Hill

Our Overnight Guest

A new baby calf was born one afternoon
Grandpa said it had been born way too soon
It was weak and he thought it would surely die
But the girls begged their Daddy – We have to try!
If we can please just keep him inside
If you will just let us– we can keep it alive
And isn't there suppose to be a snow storm
We should keep him in the kitchen – since he was just born!
To get Grandma's OK, they had to implore
So they begged and pleaded with her to let him sleep in her floor
Morning came soon and we were met with a treat!
That new baby calf was up on its feet
It had left the kitchen and was in another room
Grandma said "Now you need to get it out of there SOON!
You take it out now, right out the door
Hurry now, before it gets stuff on my floor
Well it took all three to catch and hold it tight without harm
All three of them carried it safely back to the barn
They looked at Grandma, and seeing all of them grin
She said to herself – I'm glad I gave in
If that poor little calf had been left outside
Without a doubt it surely would have died.
This memory remains with me still
From Grandpa's Farm High on the Hill

The Mouse Trap

We had a mouse, I could hear it play
I said to myself, I've got to catch it one day!
It would eat on everything in the cupboards or on the floor
So I set a trap in the dark behind a door
Between the garage and the living room
I put the trap in the corner, back behind a broom
The next day as I sat with a book in my lap
I heard a noise, it sounded like a snap
I felt so happy as I had baited the trap well
Was sure that night I'd have a story to tell
If it really was the mouse, it did not linger
For when I picked up the trap it snapped on my little finger
It wasn't the mouse trap I heard at all
It was a noise from down the hall
The next time I set a mouse trap, I will put it in plain sight
And never check it with out a light!
This not so funny memory remains with me still
From Grandpa's Farm High on the Hill

The Move

The Farm in Cushing, OK, sold in 2005
Grandpa and I thought – How can we survive
In a small space- with the noise of the cars
It's just not as peaceful as on that farm of ours
We miss the animals, the birds and the view
There are no outside chores - not much to do
Oh! We go to the store for eggs & bread
To fight all the traffic we both surely dread
Grandpa may need oil or gas for the car
But for these we don't have to go very far
The noise of the city, our days and nights fill
It makes us remember the peace & quiet we had on our hill
We may not now have all the animals, the view or the trees
But all generations to come will always have our sweet
      memories
Of Grandpa's Farm High on the Hill

The Possum

A possum came to our barn to live – yes its true!
Grandpa shook his head – not knowing just what to do
It looked so full and moved around so slow
What to do with her – he really didn't know
To shoot her – or just make her go far away
He would have to make up his mind today
She didn't seem dangerous – probably wouldn't do much
    harm
Grandpa knew for sure she couldn't live in his barn
When Grandpa was busy, she had gone outside and was
    under a tree
She had given birth to three baby possums, nursing as
    contented as could be.

The Rest of the Story

In 2005, after more than 30 years in Cushing, Oklahoma, the Kings sold "Grandpa's Farm" and moved to Stillwater, Oklahoma, where they still reside. But they will never forget "Grandpa's Farm High on the Hill" – the view, the animals and all the wonderful memories that living on our Oklahoma farm provided.

~~~~~~~~~~~~~~~~~~~~~~

They miss he farmhouse Grandpa built. It was a Spanish-Indian style home, and the barn was next to the house, with a fense running around it.

~~~~~~~~~~~~~~~~~~~~~~

They also miss the animals, like Cherokee, the horse that ran away, and Chez, the dog that saved the day.

Woodrow, or Grandpa in our story, and Juanita were married in 1946 after he came home from World War II. The picture below was taken during their honeymoon in Denver, Colorado.

www.ingramcontent.com/pod-product-compliance
Lightning Source LLC
Chambersburg PA
CBHW071753040426
42446CB00012B/2535